GIRTON COLLEGE STUDIES

EDITED BY LILIAN KNOWLES, LITT.D., READER IN ECONOMIC HISTORY
IN THE UNIVERSITY OF LONDON

No. 4.

A NEW

LAW OF THOUGHT

AND ITS LOGICAL BEARINGS

A NEW

LAW OF THOUGHT

AND ITS LOGICAL BEARINGS

BY

E. E. CONSTANCE JONES

Author of *A Primer of Logic*

WITH A PREFACE BY

PROFESSOR STOUT

"One of the greatest pains of human nature
is the pain of a new idea." BAGEHOT.

Cambridge :

at the University Press

1911

CAMBRIDGE
UNIVERSITY PRESS

University Printing House, Cambridge CB2 8BS, United Kingdom

Published in the United States of America by Cambridge University Press, New York

Cambridge University Press is part of the University of Cambridge.

It furthers the University's mission by disseminating knowledge in the pursuit of education, learning and research at the highest international levels of excellence.

www.cambridge.org
Information on this title: www.cambridge.org/9781107626652

© Cambridge University Press 1911

First published 1911
First paperback edition 2013

A catalogue record for this publication is available from the British Library

ISBN 978-1-107-62665-2 Paperback

PREFACE

TWO of the three fundamental Laws of Thought, which are traditionally regarded as the cardinal principles of Formal Logic, are concerned with the relation of propositions to each other. According to the Law of Contradiction, two propositions of the form "*A is B*" and "*A is not B*" cannot both be true. According to the Law of Excluded Middle, they cannot both be false. Now it is clear that if there is another principle which expresses the fundamental condition of the possibility of any proposition taken by itself, without reference to others, this also must be regarded as a fundamental Law of Thought, and as being logically prior to the Laws of Contradiction and Excluded Middle. It is the aim of Miss Jones in the following pages to show that there is such a Law, and to exhibit in detail its vital importance in the treatment of the whole range of topics with which Formal Logic deals. This Law of "Significant Assertion" is formulated as follows:—*Every Subject of Predication is an identity (of denotation) in diversity (of intension).* In other words, every affirmative proposition asserts, and every negative proposition denies, the union of different attributes within the unity of the same thing. In every affirmative proposition, the subject-term designates something as characterised in one way, and the predicate designates the same thing as characterised in another way. This Law of Significant Assertion is substituted by Miss Jones for the traditional Law of Identity, as expressed in the formula "*A is A.*" "*A is A*," if it has any significance at all, must, she holds, be taken as an attempt to express the essential nature of all predication; but so regarded it is plainly untenable; for to say "*A is A*" is merely to say "*A*" twice, and not to assert anything about "*A.*" There is no proposition, unless what is characterised as "*A*" in the subject-term is also characterised as "*B*" in the predicate-term.

The service which Miss Jones has rendered to Logic in this little volume lies not so much in the mere enunciation of the "Law of Significant Assertion" as in her thorough and systematic application of it, so as to clear up special logical problems. By way of illustration, I may refer to her discussion of the doctrine of "the fourfold implication of propositions in Connotation and Denotation," and to her account of immediate inferences, and of the syllogism. As regards syllogistic inference, it may be worth while to refer to a point which Miss Jones has not expressly noticed. The Law of Significant Assertion supplies the most direct, simple and general vindication of the syllogism against the charge of *petitio principii.* The charge is based on the fact that the conclusion asserts of the same thing the same predicate which has already been ascribed to it in the major premiss. The straightforward reply is, that in the conclusion this predicate is brought into connexion with an attribute with which it has not been connected in either of the premisses. *A*

remarks to B, " That woman in the corner is a scare-crow."
B replies, " Sir, that woman is my wife." For A, it is a
startling novelty, and no mere repetition, to discover that
he has called B's wife a scare-crow. The novelty is plainly
due to a new synthesis of attributes with the same denotation, the combination of the attribute of being B's wife
with that of being the woman whom A has just called a
scare-crow.

Miss Jones seems to have made out a good case for
regarding the Law of Significant Assertion as a fundamental Law of Thought. But its claim to be the only
justifiable rendering of the Law of Identity is not so
clear. The best writers on Logic tend to interpret this
law as expressing the immutability of truth. According
to them, it means that the truth of a proposition is
unaffected by variation of time, place and circumstances,
or of the minds which apprehend it. Either this principle, or, if the pragmatists be right, its contradictory,
seems to demand recognition as a fundamental law of
thought, and it is certainly a principle of Identity. But
it is of course no substitute for the Law of Significant
Assertion. The question which of the two is the most
appropriate interpretation of the cryptic formula "A is A"
is of quite subordinate interest.

G. F. STOUT.

St Andrews.
March, 1911.

CONTENTS

INTRODUCTORY SUMMARY

My object in the following brief essay is to propound a certain analysis of Categorical Propositions of the forms *S is P, S is not P,* to show that this is the only general analysis which it is possible to accept, and to indicate its bearing upon logical science. According to the analysis in question, *S is P* asserts Identity of Denotation in Diversity of Intension, and *S is not P* denies this. The example given by Professor Frege (whose analysis of *S is P* I understand to agree roughly with mine) is

"The morning star is the evening star" $\left(\substack{\text{M. S.} \\ \text{E. S.}}\right)$: the

terms "morning star" and "evening star" apply to *one thing,* but the meaning, intension, or qualitative implication of "morning star" is not the same as that of "evening star." "The largest city in the world is the Metropolis of England" is another illustration, where again it is clear that the two names or terms, the Subject and Predicate of the Assertion, apply to *one place* but have different meanings or definitions. *S is not P* asserts Difference of Denotation (Otherness) in Difference of Intension (Diversity)—e.g. "Cambridge is not Oxford,"

$\left(\text{C}\right)\left(\text{O}\right)$. *A is related to B* implies *A is not B,*

$\left(\text{A}\right)\left(\text{B}\right)$.

We need propositions of the form *S is P, S is not P*, for significant assertion, and without them no satisfactory statement can be given of the " three fundamental Laws of Thought," which are put forward as the basis of logical science. The first two of these Laws are commonly formulated as: (1) *A is A*, (2) *A is not non-A*, and the third sometimes as *A is either A or non-A* (3). Desperate efforts have been made by logicians to give a valuable meaning to *A is A* ; but if *A is A*, interpreted as *A is A*, is retained as the first fundamental Law, there is no possible passage from it to *A is B*, and *A is A* or *A is B* (*S is P*) must be given up. This is fully recognised by Lotze, who gives up (theoretically) *S is P*. *A is A* tells us no more than *A is A*, and if we begin with it, we must also end with it, if we are to be consistent. I maintain that we must not begin with it, but must begin instead with a Law of significant assertion—assertion of the forms *S is P, S is not P*, forms which provide the only straightforward and effective statement of the second and third Laws of Thought, thus :

S is P ⎰cannot both be true (L. of Contradiction)
S is not P ⎱cannot both be false (L. of Excluded Middle).

It follows from these two Laws that of any Subject of Predication (*S*) either *P* or *not-P* can be affirmed. Thus from them, and *S is P, S is not P*, analysed as above, we obtain the principle that :

Every Subject of Predication is an Identity-in-Diversity.

It follows further that every Predicate (*P*) is necessarily incompatible with *not-P* (absence of intension *P*) and necessarily compatible with *not-not-P*. (This suggests a formal principle of necessary connection of attributes.)

I contend that if we start, not with *A is A*, but with the principle that *Every Subject of Predication is an identity (of denotation) in diversity (of intension)*, this Law (1), and the Laws of (2) Contradiction and (3) Excluded Middle (of which (1) for the first time makes logically possible the formulation given above) do furnish a real and adequate and obvious basis and starting-point of "Formal" Logic. Granted propositions of the form *S is P*, with the identity-in-diversity analysis and the corresponding analysis of *S is not P*, together with the traditional Laws of Contradiction and Excluded Middle, the whole scheme of Immediate and Mediate Inference can be built up systematically and explicitly, as I hope to show. The possibility of Conversion, e.g. implies that the Predicate, as well as the Subject, of any Proposition has Denotation, and a Denotation that is implicitly quantified; the one indispensable condition of Mediate Inference is identity of Denotation of the Middle Term in both premisses. Without propositions of the forms *S is P*, *S is not P*, thought cannot live or move; but the disastrous acceptance of *A is A*, with its baffling ambiguities, has stood in the way of their being rightly analysed by logicians and explicitly recognised by them as fundamental forms of significant assertion, without which not even the Laws of Contradiction and Excluded Middle can receive satisfactory expression[1].

---

[1] In the following pages I have occasionally borrowed from writings of my own in cases where I have not felt able to improve upon the statement already printed.

A NEW "LAW OF THOUGHT" AND ITS LOGICAL BEARINGS

"I am the pillars of the house,
The keystone of the arch am I;
Take me away, and roof and wall
Would fall to ruin utterly."

K. Tynan.

STATEMENT OF THE CASE.

It will be admitted that up to the present time no adequate and unquestionable basis of the Science of Logic has been found—that the Method of Logic, itself the Science of Method, is not wholly satisfactory. Logic is often defined as the Science of the Laws of Thought— the Laws, that is, of Identity, Contradiction, and Excluded Middle; but on the one hand the statement of these Laws is not uniform, and the interpretation of at least the first of them, the Law of Identity (*A is A*, whatever is is, Everything is what it is), is matter of perpetual dispute; on the other hand no one of these Laws alone, nor all of them together, can or do take account of, or can explain and justify, the common indispensable form of Categorical Assertion *S is P*—e.g. Trees are green, All Men are mortal, George V is the present King of England, Perseverance is admirable, Honesty is the best policy, The quality of Mercy is twice bless'd. On the contrary, *A is A* appears to exclude it, and there is no passage from *A is A* to *A is B*. And if anyone who accepts *A is A*, and the corresponding expression of the Law of Contradiction, *A is not not-A*, is driven into giving *A is B or not-B* as the Law of Excluded Middle, it is for him to show what logical connexion there is between the last "Law" and the two previous ones. Logic undoubtedly, like all other Sciences, like literature, like common thought and common speech, uses the forms *S is P, S is not P*—uses them at every step. It must use them, of course; it has no choice; without them, it would be impossible to affirm or deny; but it adopts them in the same fashion as Bentham adopted the *Greatest Happiness of the Greatest number* as his ultimate ethical principle—that is to say, without any reasoned justification. No "plain man" certainly, would be expected to give any reason why he should use propositions of the form *A is B* rather than of the form *A is A*; but a logician who declares that *A is A* is the first Law of Thought, and (if he is consistent), that *A is not not-A* and *A is either A or not A*[1] are the other two, may fairly be called upon to explain the fact that he habitually says that Roses are red and Violets are blue, rather than Roses are roses, Red is red, Violets are violets, and so on. For logicians to find fault with a so-called "Law" which is a pure tautology, which is expressed in a form which may indeed have important uses, and may be employed epigrammatically or rhetorically, but in which no ordinary sensible person would think of trying to convey straightforward information, or matter of fact— much less a fundamental principle—is no new thing.

---

[1] This, however, is generally stated *A is either B or not B* and sometimes the *A is B* form is slipped into even in stating the Law of Contradiction, by upholders of the *A is A* Law of Identity.

To lay it down (1) that we can never legitimately affirm
of any subject a predicate different from itself, while at
the same time (2) it has to be allowed that this rule
cannot be even stated without being broken, without
using assertions of the form *S is P*, was we know, a state
of mind possible in the time of Plato; it was possible
because those who asserted (1) thought it self-evident
that the Predicate ought always to be the same as its
Subject, "that to apply many Predicates to one and the
same Subject is to make one thing into many things."
And as for (2), they could not deny it; while to give
up (1) seemed to be a denial of self-evident truth, to give
up (2) was sheerly impossible. The situation is rather
intolerable.

That there is a difficulty about *S is P* we need not
question, that logicians who accept *A is A* are impera-
tively called upon to show how this "Law" can be adapted
to propositions of form *A is B* (*S is P*) is too obvious
to need pointing out. Some writers have tried to give a
meaning to *A is A* which does not seem to prohibit
diversity of Predicate from Subject—a meaning which
is itself expressed in the *A is B*, not in the tautological
A is A, form ; Mr Bradley e.g. interprets the Law of
Identity to mean that "if what I say is really true, it
stands for ever." *A is A* thus expounded into *A is B*
does not of course exclude propositions of *A is B* form.
Dr Bosanquet frankly admits that, while he would not
accept either *A is B* or *A is A* as a schematic expression of the Law of Identity, he would prefer *A is B*
to *A is A*[1].

[1] "If I were asked" he says, "how I should represent a true
Identity, such as a judgment must express, in a schematic form with

The only logician, as far as I know, who, while re-taining *A is A* in its purity has made a determined effort to reconcile it with propositions of the *A is B* (*S is P*) form, is Lotze. He holds (*Logic*, Bk I. ch. II.) that "our thought is subject to a limitation, has to conform to a law...in the categorical judgment each constituent can only be conceived as self-same [= ?]. This primary law of thought, the *principle of identity*, we express positively in the formula *A = A*." He states the conclusion to

symbolic letters, I should say the problem was insoluble. Every A is B would be much better than Every A is A; but as the letters are not parts in any whole of meaning, they are 'things cut asunder with an axe'." (Dr Bosanquet in *Mind*, 1888, p. 357.) (The objection that in *A is B* "the letters are not parts in any whole of meaning" seems either

(1) inaccurate, for there is a symbolic whole, viz. $\overparen{A, B,}$ which has

a meaning and an important one,—or (2) irrelevant, if what is meant is a concrete special "whole of meaning.")

It is clear from other passages in the same article that for Dr Bosanquet, individual identity is not distinguished from *qualitative one-ness of two things*—e.g., he speaks of some "present impression" as being "identical with a former impression" (p. 360), and says that "the element of *identity* between two outlines can be accurately pointed out and limited, but the moment they cease to be two, it ceases to be an identity" (p. 359). He objects to drawing "a sharp line between the unity of the individual human being...and the unity of human beings in identical sentiments, ideas, purposes or habits" (p. 362), and says that a number of persons may have "a really *identical* purpose and endeavour and *consciousness* of certain facts" (p. 364). Again (p. 365), he says " Any indiscernible resemblance [= ?] between two different contents, in specified respects, will do whatever identity will do, because it is identity under another name " (if so, what need is there of a Distributed Middle in Syllogism?); and on p. 366 speaks of "indis-cernible likeness [= ?] or identity." With this meaning of identity it certainly is not clear how "a true identity" could be satisfactorily expressed as *A is B*. Connotationally, qualitatively, *A is not B.*

which he is driven, thus: "This absolute connexion of two concepts S and P, in which the one is unconditionally the other and yet both stand over against each other as different, is a relation quite impracticable in thought: by means of *this* copula, the simple 'is' of the categorical judgment, two different contents cannot be connected at all; they must either fall entirely within one another, or they must remain entirely separate, and the impossible judgment 'S *is* P' resolves itself into the three others, 'S *is* S,' 'P *is* P,' 'S *is not* P'." (Engl. transl. p. 59.)

Whether A *is* A is understood as A-*ness is* A-*ness*, or in any other possible way in which A *is* A is honestly interpreted as A *is* A (not as A *is* B), the acceptance of it as a first and fundamental Law is absolutely suicidal for Logic from a theoretical point of view. But it must be confessed that its nominal acceptance does not appear to have seriously affected the construction of the Science. A *is* A cannot justify or support this, it even seems inconsistent with it, but the restrictions logically imposed by A *is* A have (almost universally) been not only not respected, they have not even been borne in mind, and A *is* A itself has received a variety of interpretations (generally of the form A *is* B) which it was natural to ignore as they mostly did not interfere with either theory or practice, and it was thus easy for logicians to go on systematising and constructing in complete independence of the "First Law of Thought."

No doubt the speculative incompatibility between it and ordinary assertion has been for the most part a "contradiction that was not seen." When it has been seen, common sense has had no hesitation in driving a coach-

and-six through the venerable but insubstantial obstacle. Lotze, keenly aware of the contradiction and loyal to tradition, but oblivious for the moment of the needs and actualities of living thought, imagined that he must, and could, give up S *is* P. The actual starting-point of Logic has been not A *is* A, but the Law of Contradiction and the Law of Excluded Middle, and the effort to analyse S *is* P (*not-P*); and in Conversion, Mediate Inference etc., it is propositions of those forms that have been dealt with. But those forms were accepted uncritically, and together with A *is* A. Logic has lacked a First Law which could furnish a legitimate and logical starting-point and be capable of development and general application, have a real and important difference from, and connexion with, the Law of Contradiction and the Law of Excluded Middle, be effective throughout the Science of Logic, and justify, explain and support logical procedure. Though A *is* A may be sometimes a convenient mode of expression, we cannot start from it as the fundamental propositional form and we do not see how to get from it to A *is* B. A *is* B is the inevitable point of departure, and this has, as the limit on one side (the side of tautology) A *is* A (which excludes diversity of intension), and on the other (the side of Contradiction), A *is* *not-A* (which excludes identity of denotation). A *is* A, $\left(\text{A, A} \right)$, is of course quite different from $A = A$, $\left(\text{A} \right) = \left(\text{A.} \right)$.

I think that every name or term has two aspects:

    (1) the denotational, extensional, or applicational;

    (2) the intensional or connotational;

corresponding to the two aspects of the things of which they are names—i.e. the aspects of (1) Thatness and (2) Whatness, to use Mr Bradley's terms. Everything of which we can think or speak is (1) Something and (2) some definite sort of something. Everything must be thought as having (1) existence (in the widest sense— mere thing-hood) and (2) some fixed definite nature and constitution. For the sake of clearness, I propose in what follows to confine the term *identity* to denotational one- ness, as distinct from one-ness in the intensional sense, which makes possible general names, classing, and classi- fication. Without both (1) and (2) no assertion is possible, nothing can be Subject or Predicate of a proposition, The Law of Identity may have been an attempt to express the qualitative fixity of nature of anything in brief and self-evident form; if so, the expression *A is A* is unfortunately incapable of expressing what was in- tended. If it does express a meaning, that meaning is clearly not self-evident, for there is nothing about which there has been more dispute than the meaning of *A is A*. It seems to me that until we have *A is B* (*S is P*) there is nothing to accept or reject, nothing to doubt or dispute, and that the true significance of contradiction is to deny of something some predicate which has already been affirmed of it. It might seem that for conceptualists the problem of *A is A* was simplified, as their whole interest was in Quality, Intension, as distinct from Extension or Thatness; but it is demonstrable that no significant affirmation can be purely qualitative.

    If we genuinely accept *A is A* as the expression of a fundamental and primary logical principle, the difficulty is, how theoretically to get beyond it. If we reject it, what we need, and what we find, to put in its place, is a principle of significant Assertion—Assertion of the form *S is P*. The laws of Contradiction and Excluded Middle are laws of the *relations* of assertions, and they cannot be expressed in satisfactory and unambiguous form without the use of *S is P*, *S is not P*, propositions. So even for them we require a prior principle, explaining and justifying the *S is P* proposition itself. Such a logical principle, based on a new analysis of *S is P*, I think I can provide.

I call the analysis in question "new" because although I put it forward in print in 1890, and although Dr Keynes in his *Formal Logic* has practically adopted it as appropriate to "logical equations" (*loc. cit.* 4th edit. pp. 189, 190), it has not received much attention—no doubt because many other accounts of the Categorical Proposition have looked so like it (and in fact sometimes came so near it) that the fundamental difference has not been recognised.

> "Oh, the little more and how much it is,
> And the little less and what worlds away."

And although my own conviction has remained unshaken because the doctrine has seemed to me to stand all the tests that I could apply in a thoroughly satisfactory manner, I should not have taken up the question again at this time but for two circumstances. One is that I have rather suddenly become aware that my analysis furnishes a law of Categorical Assertion which together with the Laws of Contradiction and Excluded Middle stated in *S is P*, *S is not P*, form does provide Formal Logic with an adequate foundation, and gives a systematising principle, in complete accord both with common thought and common usage, and with the accepted structure of logical science, and is perhaps further of direct philosophical importance.

The other circumstance to which I refer is, that I have recently had my attention drawn to the fact that Professor Frege's analysis of Categoricals (published in 1892) was apparently the same as my own, and that a similar view was adopted by Mr B. Russell (1903) in his *Principles of Mathematics*, where Frege's theory of the import of propositions is expounded with sympathetic approbation.

Recognising in Terms the two aspects of Extension (or Denotation) and Intension (as Jevons and most other modern writers on Logic do), I approach from that point of view the question : How are the propositions of the forms *S is P*, *S is not P*, to be analysed ?—I hold that one or other of these two symbolic expressions may be applied to every Categorical Proposition. Further, that in Propositions of which the Term-names are Class-names—e.g. All Lions are carnivora—conversion, involving Quantification of the Predicate, is possible and legitimate.

By the Extension or Denotation of a Term I mean the things to which it applies, by its Intension I mean those properties or qualities of the things which it signifies. As Dr Keynes says : " The *extension* of a name consists of objects of which the name can be predicated; its intension consists of properties which can be predicated of it " (*Formal Logic*, 4th ed. p. 22). " Intension may be used to indicate in the most general way what may be called the implicational aspect of names " (*loc. cit.* p. 26). E.g. (1) *Quadruped* in extension denotes lions, tigers, horses, dogs, kittens, etc., etc., in intension it means *having four feet*; *gold* in extension applies to this cup, that ring, those sovereigns, etc., in intension it means yellow, heavy, malleable, insoluble in *aqua regia* ; *man* in extension denotes Henri Bergson, Josiah Royce, J. J. Sargent, Mary Findlater, Jane Barlow, Madame Curie, etc., in intension it signifies *having rationality and animality*.

It is to be observed that we may know the application or extension of a name and not know its intension (definition or signification) and *vice versa*. E.g. I know that metal in extension denotes gold, silver, copper, iron, lead, tin, mercury, aluminium, etc., and I know these when I see them, but I am not able to give a satisfactory statement of the intension which they have in common.

Or again I know, or I may know, all the inhabitants of a country parish and be able to greet them correctly by name when I meet them, but may be entirely unable to give a recognisable description of any of them. Or I may know real diamonds from paste, or one disease from another, and always apply the names rightly, and yet be unable to set out even to myself the connotation or intension.

On the other hand I may have full descriptive knowledge of a person or plant or precious stone, and yet not be able to recognise the person or plant or jewel though it may much concern me to do so. I may even know much more about a person than his ordinary acquaintances, or even than his dearest friend, and be able to give a much more accurate description of his appearance and manner, and yet not know him when I meet him. Or I may recognise, though I cannot define, Justice ; and define, though I might not recognise, a chiliagon.

Extension and Intension or both may be imaginary. I may put together elements universally recognised as charming, and draw a fancy portrait or a fictitious character; or I may attribute to an actual person impossible or incompatible perfections.

What I insist on is that all the names we use have both Extension and Intension ; and either of these may be a guide to the other. I may have the things to which a name applies put before me (Extensive definition) and from examination of them reach the intension: or have intension given, and go out and by means of it determine extension.

It may occasionally be possible and be convenient to apply the terms Extension, Intension, to *things* as well as to their *names*, but I suggest as generally appropriate to *things* and not names, the terms Quiddity and Quality for the aspects of Thatness and Whatness in things, and Entity for Quiddity+Quality, and for *that which is asserted* in a proposition as distinct from the *assertion*, I would suggest the term *Assertum*.

According to my analysis, propositions of the form *S is P* assert *identity of denotation (extension) in diversity of intension* (S̲ P̲) ; while correspondingly *S is not P* asserts *difference (or otherness) of denotation in intensional diversity* (S̲)(P̲)—i.e. it denies identity of denotation. In *S is not P* the intension of *P* is asserted to be absent from what is denoted by *S.* The purpose of *S is not P* is not to assert that the intension of *S* is diverse from the intension of *P*—that goes without saying, and is essential to *S is P.* The speaker who asserts *S is P* starts from a whole (S P) ; the hearer or learner hears first S, then P, and puts the two together into the whole, (S P) , from which the speaker started. The *is* of the S *is* P cannot mean sameness of intension (exact similarity) for S and P *ex vi terminorum* are diverse, have different intensions—as Lotze avows (cp. *ante*), two different concepts or contents cannot be connected at all by the simple " is " of the categorical judgment; if S and P were taken in intension only, we could say of S nothing but that S *is not* P; and if S *is* P did not indicate one-ness of denotation, then S and P would not refer to an identical object, and we should again have to say S *is not* P. If terms were taken in denotation only, we should not know what to do with more than one Term in affirmation.

An intension S neither (1) excludes from the denotation of S every other intension P, nor (2) does the addition of P to S *change* the intension S. If (1), no significant affirmation would be possible; if (2), we should never be sure *what* we were affirming. The *thing* which is S is of course modified by the addition to it of the intension P, but not so the *intension* S.

"Suppose I assert that *all fronds of the Mountain Buckler are erect.* The meaning of the assertion is fixed and definite, and, if true, it is true once for all. If I go on to say that the fronds are also lance-shaped in form, pinnately divided, that the pinnae stand opposite (generally), that they are narrow and tapering and are pinnatifidly divided—do any of these affirmations, or all of them, in the least alter or modify the meaning of my original statement that all the fronds are erect? It must be admitted that no one of them alters the meaning of any other; but what *is* very importantly modified is my knowledge of, and power of 'identifying,' the thing itself, the actual object in time and space, the Subject of Attributes to which all these successive characteristics are assigned. All the successive predicates are related as joint characteristics of the whole which they qualify; they are related not as modifying each other, but as modifying it.

That the interior angles of an isosceles triangle are equal to two right-angles, is a general truth, the meaning of which is not affected by the further general truth that the angles at the base of an isosceles triangle are equal to each other, or that any triangle is half of a parallelogram. The meaning of the assertion: This is an engraving of a picture by Gainsborough, is not modified or changed by the further assertions: The picture is a portrait of Lady Mulgrave, it is one of the artist's masterpieces, it is supposed to be now in America. But though any one of these statements does not alter or modify the meaning of the others, each one does modify the hearer's knowledge *concerning the object which is spoken of.*" (*Mind*, 1908, p. 391, etc.)

Propositions of forms *S is P, S is not P* having been admitted, and analysed as above (pp. 14, 15), we are of course justified in formulating the commonly accepted logical Laws of Contradiction and Excluded Middle as follows:

S *is* P } cannot both be true (Law of Contradiction.
S *is not* P } cannot both be false (Law of Excluded Middle).

Both these Laws appear to be self-evident, and it is perhaps partly because A *is* A has been supposed to be self-evident κατ' ἐξοχήν, that it has so long held its ground, and that such persevering and desperate efforts have been made to give it an interpretation which would fit it for the post of the First Law of Thought. If Logic were provided with laws really self-evident, laws also on which the Science could be based, and according to which its structure could be built up,—then indeed the foundation and method of Logic would be adequate and satisfactory. The old Law of Identity, however, affords only a simulacrum of self-evidence. The Law of Identity in Diversity which I propose to put in its place is simply a law of significant assertion—a law which while it is arrived at through analysis of propositions of the form *S is P* (*S is not P*) implies conditions which make such assertions possible, conditions without which knowledge itself seems impossible—without assertions of this form, knowledge could not be communicated, nor even formulated. I hold that there is no alternative and really primary analysis which will bear investigation; that all valid interpretations of categoricals which go beyond this must be based upon it.

That *S is P* asserts an Identity of Extension in Diversity of Intension seems to me to be on reflection self-evident. I should at any rate claim that its denial must be admitted to be inconceivable, and as to the form *S is P*, as the Eleatic Stranger in the *Sophistes* observed, men " admit it implicitly and involuntarily in their common forms of speech, they cannot carry on a conversation without it."

Taking together the three Laws of Identity in Diversity, of Contradiction, and of Excluded Middle, we may say that of any Subject (*S*), *P* must be affirmed or denied, but not both, i.e. of any subject (*S*), *P*, or *not-P*, but not both, can be predicated. Thus we reach the principle that

Any Subject of Predication is an identity of denotation in diversity of intension.

Such subject is a whole to which the two terms S and P (or not-P) are applicable as names. For every S is P, (S P) , or *not-P*, (Snot-P) ; to the thing spoken of, in both cases, diverse intensions, S and P, or S and not-P, are assigned, and S and P (or not-P) are equally names of the denotational whole (S P) (or (Snot-P)), and are therefore interchangeable, and can be substituted one for the other. The Law of Identity just formulated implies, I believe, that

Everything is an identity of extension in diversity of intension.

At any rate we could only disprove this by showing that there is something which is *not* a Subject of Predication. But to show this, we must expressly treat it as a Subject of Predication. Thus the proof that it is *not*, involves that it *is*. Everything is a possible Subject of Predication, and, directly the question is raised, it becomes an actual Subject of Predication.

In the Law of Contradiction what is asserted is, that if the diverse intensions signified by S and P are identical in denotation, (S P) , then the diverse intensions S, and not-P (absence of intension P), are not identical in denotation (S) (not-P) . What the Law of Excluded

Middle asserts is that if the intensions signified by S and P (or not-P) have not identical denotation, then the intensions S and not-P (or P) have identical denotation. P, and not-P (= intension P absent), are mutually exclusive, and together exhaustive of all possibilities.

Though *S is P* is not a self-evident and universally applicable proposition, *S is P or not-P* is both, but we should not have been in a position to assert it, unless we had first established the forms *S is P, S is not P*. If it were inevitable to analyse *S is P* as Lotze feels forced to do into:

S is S,
P is P,
S is not P,

no such principle could be formulated.

S is P, S is not P, express the two kinds or qualities of assertion, affirmative and negative, in the most general and abstract way, as $a = b$ may stand for any and every equation.

There are large and important groups of assertions which though they can be expressed as *S is P* are more appropriately exhibited in skeleton form and diagrammatically as *A is not B*, (A) (B), since what they affirm is a relation between two things which have not identical extension, however vital the relation between them may be.

E.g., *A* is equal to *B*, *C* is father of *D*, *E* is to the left of *F*:

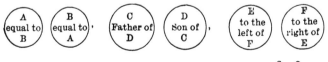

2—2

In $A = B$ there is between A and B equality of quantity or value in intensional diversity—i.e., there is not only denotational identity, but also qualitative sameness in qualitative diversity.

In all the above instances two non-identical things are considered in their relation to each other, in the "system" of related things (numbers or quantities, family connexions, positions in space) to which they respectively belong. But the matter of fact in each case can be perfectly well expressed (in any given case) as an identity in diversity—thus:

A is equal-to-B, E is to-the-left-of-F, and so on.

A *is not* B and E *is not* F, and it cannot be predicated of A that it is B, nor of E that it is F; but we can predicate of A that it is *something equal to B*, of E that it is *something to the left of F*.

The copula in : A is equal-to-B,
E is to-the-left-of-F
(as always in *S is P* propositions) signifies identity of denotation, and the *special kind of relation* between A and B, E and F is here expressed *in the Predicate*.

In dealing with any " Relative Propositions," a knowledge of the special system to which they belong is required. The symbolic forms *S is P*, *S is not P*, are the only ones that can be applied everywhere, and as they are of the extremest generality, they are also of the extremest abstractness and simplicity. The Subject and Predicate in any *S is P* give the whole (S̲ P) from which it is inferrible that P is S, not-P is not-S, not-S is not-P. *S is not P* gives the "system" (S) (P), from which it can be inferred that P is not S, not-S is P, not-P is S. Of course every variety of systematic relation between S and P is possible, as has just been indicated.

A fortiori arguments are simply a special case of arguments which turn upon Relativity of Terms.

A Proposition which has a relative term for S or P or both, besides the ordinary Immediate Inferences (Eductions) which can be drawn from it in just the same way as from non-relative Propositions, furnishes other immediate inferences to anyone acquainted with the system to which it refers. These inferences cannot be educed except by a person knowing the "system"; on the other hand, no knowledge is needed of the objects referred to, except a knowledge of their place in the system, and this knowledge is in many cases co-extensive with ordinary intelligence; consider, e.g., the relations of magnitude of objects in space, of the successive parts of time, of family connexions, of number. From such a Proposition as: *C is a grandfather of D*, in addition to such inferences as could be drawn from a non-relative Proposition (a-grandfather-of-D is C, not-a-grandfather-of-D is not-C, etc.), it is, of course, possible for anyone having the most elementary knowledge of family relationship to infer further that:

D is a grandchild of C,

A parent of D is a child of C,

A child of D is a great-grandchild of C,

The father of C is a great-grandfather of D, etc.

From C is equal to D (besides Something equal to D is
C, No not-equal to D is C, etc.), it can be inferred that

D is equal to C,
C is not less than D,
D is not greater than C,
C is not greater than D,
Whatever is greater than C is
    greater than D,

and so on (compare C is an inference from D).

In each of the above examples we are not dealing with
one object or group in the same way as in non-relative
Propositions, e.g.,

All men are
    mortal,
Byzantium is
    Constantinople,
This bird is a lark;

but we are considering, besides the identity of application of S and P, two objects denotationally distinct,
namely C and D. (See my *General Logic*, p. 34.)

If, making an advance in complication, and passing to
Mediate Inference, it is asserted that:

M is P
and S is M,

the hearer is entitled to the construction (S M P) , where

three diverse intensions are referred to one denotation;
and each of the terms M, P, S, applies to, is a name of,

the whole (S,M,P) , and each one may be asserted of either

of the others. Thus this construction entitles the hearer to the assertion *S is P*, which had not been actually asserted. The speaker who asserted first *M is P*, and then *S is M*, must have had before him *at starting* the whole (S M P), which his hearer reached as a result of putting together *M is P*, *S is M*.

Thus the conditions of affirmative Mediate Inference with S, M, and P as terms may be formulated as follows: If the denotation of any two terms, M and P, is identical, any third Term S, which is identical in denotation with either of them, is also identical in denotation with the other. If in accordance with this pronouncement I reach a whole of denotation which has intensions M, P, and S, thus (S M P), it is obvious that I am as much entitled to assert identity of denotation between S and P as between M and P or S and M.

For negative Mediate Inference with Terms, *S*, *M*, *P* the following canon may be suggested:

If of two terms *S*, *P*, one is, and one is not, identical in denotation with a third Term *M*; then *S* and *P* are not identical in denotation.

Hypotheticals are all either (1) Immediate Inferences (e.g., If M is P, P is M), or Mediate Inferences which are (2) fully expressed (e.g., If M is P, and S is M, then S is P)—which like (1) may be called Self-contained; or (3) Mediate Inferences which are elliptical and enthymematic—e.g. If M is P, S is P (∵ S is M), If A is B, E is F (∵ B is C, and C is D, and D is E); If S is M, S is P (∵ M is P); If S is M, S is not P (∵ M is not P).

Conditionals (as distinguished by Dr Keynes and

Mr Johnson from Hypotheticals) are merely Categoricals with a Subject-Term which is resolvable into Genus + Differentia, expressed in Hypothetical form because the Predicate is limited to that part of the Class or Genus which is qualified or conditioned by the Differentia. E.g. If any triangle is equilateral, it is equiangular—equiangularity in a triangle follows from, depends upon, is inseparable from, its equilaterality. A Hypothetical, like an Inference, must start from something *given* (a proposition or propositions). Inferences can be put in hypothetical form, and Hypotheticals in inferential form.

I will examine concrete examples later, but may observe here that there are some propositions—Categorical, Hypothetical, and Alternative—which seem to be used as a rhetorical device; e.g., If Newton was not a greater mathematician than Kepler, the whole is not greater than the part, We are the victims of misunderstanding, or the truth is not true. These only amount to a very strong asseveration (1) that Newton was greater than Kepler; (2) that we are the victims of misunderstanding. We can, no doubt, and do, use propositional forms in cases where instead of the *form* (S is P, etc.) resulting naturally from the *content*, the only connection of content is that imposed by the form (S is P, If A is B, C is D, etc.) upon an indifferent or even recalcitrant content: E.g., we may

give the form *S is P* to an *A not-A* $\overparen{\left(A\,not\text{-}A \right)}$ content, as

in the above examples (the whole is not greater than the part, the truth is not true).

In the above brief and simple statement is contained, I believe, the essential framework of the theory of Import of Categorical assertions of forms *S is P*, *S is not P*, of Hypothetical assertion, of Immediate Inference, and Mediate Inference. The expansion and complication introduced by its application to Class-Propositions will be considered forthwith. Here I will only remark that the twofold relation (affirmative and negative) of Subject and Predicate in assertion (which must be distinguished from the relation between Subject and Attribute) is quite disparate from the fivefold relation possible between two classes taken in extension, and no theory of the one can be made perfectly symmetrical with any theory of the other.

It is, I think, to the prominence given to Class-Propositions and the predominant use of such Propositions as examples (whether symbolic or significant) in books of Logic, that the blurring of the clear and simple outlines of Assertion (affirmative and negative) is largely due.

Such propositions as R is Q, Tully is Cicero, Courage is Valour, Generosity is not Justice, London is the largest city in the world, convert quite simply into : The largest city in the world is London, Justice is not Generosity, etc.

In dealing with ordinary class-propositions with quantified Subject and unquantified Predicate, the matter becomes more elaborate, and mistake more possible, because in conversion the unexpressed but implied Quantification (All, Some) of the old Predicate-name has to be expressed, since that name is now the Subject-Term; and on the other hand the expressed quantification (all, some) of the old Subject-name sinks into mere implicitness, that name being the new Predicate-name. Further, when a class-name occurs as Term without quantification, a different quantification is understood, when it is a Subject-Term, from what is understood when it is a Predicate-Term. E.g., in Trees are plants, Trees would be quantified by *all*. In Cedars are trees, trees would be quantified by *some*. And if we converted this last proposition, it would be to: Some Trees are Cedars.

Propositions of the A, E, I, O form commonly have some sign of quantity attached to the Subject and not to the Predicate, and are said to have a quantified Subject and an unquantified Predicate. It has been held by certain reformers in Logic that all Predicates are naturally quantified in thought, and ought to be explicitly quantified in speech. This view does not seem to be borne out by reflection; but careful reflection does appear to show that Quantification is an indispensable instrument of Conversion.

The place of Quantification in Logic is very curious, its function being often as completely hidden from those whose processes of Conversion involve it, as the subterranean course of a train in one of the loop-tunnels of the Swiss Alps would be to an observer who only saw it rush into one opening, and emerge again in a few minutes from another, just above or just below. My meaning will be best elucidated by taking an ordinary proposition and tracing the changes which it undergoes in Conversion.

Let the proposition be—

All human beings are rational (1)

The ordinary converse of this is—

Some rational creatures are human beings (2),

or—

Some rational creatures are human (3).

[All] human
[beings]
[some] rational
[creatures]

If I merely alter the relative position of S and P in (1) as it stands, and say—

Rational are all human beings,

it is clear that Conversion in the logical sense has not taken place; for *Rational* is still the Predicate, and *all human beings* is still the Subject. The proposition has been merely turned round. But it may be put into the form—

All human beings are rational creatures (4),

and with this we can deal. It is not, however, any more than the adjectival (1), directly convertible. If altered into—

Rational creatures are all human beings,

the proposition thus obtained, besides being awkward, is ambiguous—it is by no means clear which term is to be taken as Subject, and the *all* might even be understood to qualify (or quantify) *Rational creatures.*

The first step towards real Conversion is taken when we pass from (4) to the quantificated proposition—

All human beings are some rational creatures (5).

From this we go on to the quantificated converse—

Some rational creatures are all human beings (6);

and from (6) to the unquantificated converse of (5)—

Some rational creatures are human beings (7).

From (7) we can pass to the corresponding adjectival Proposition

Some rational creatures are human (8).

It is to be observed that in going from (4) to (7), we have not only inserted a sign of quantity before the new Subject-name (rational creatures) which, as the old Predicate, had not any to start with: we have also dropped the sign of quantity which the new Predicate (human beings) had when it was the old Subject-name. Thus, as we began with an unquantificated proposition, so we end with an unquantificated proposition. The propositions which logicians (on the whole) have recognised and dealt with are unquantificated propositions; it is for enabling us to pass (by an elliptical procedure) *from* unquantificated *to* unquantificated propositions that the ordinary rules of Conversion and Reduction of Class-Propositions and Syllogisms are framed; it is of unquantificated propositions that the "nineteen valid moods" of the traditional Categorical Syllogism are composed.

In converting an E proposition, we should proceed as follows:—Let the proposition to be converted be, No R is Q (1). (1) = (2) Any R is not Q (by grammatical equivalence). Quantificating (2) we get, Any R is not any Q (3). (3) converts to, Any Q is not any R (4). By disquantificating (4) we reach (5), Any Q is not R. And (5) = No Q is R (by grammatical equivalence).

My view then is that the usage of Logic and of ordinary speech is on the whole to be justified, and yet that Quantification is possible and valid in a subordinate office, as a necessary transformation stage of propositions. This can be made clear by reference to the Import of Categorical Propositions. What a Categorical proposition affirms or denies is, *identity of denotation* of the S and the P in *diversity of intension*. Denotation of S and of P in an affirmative Categorical Proposition are the same; intension of the S and P being, of course, always diverse in propositions of the form *S is P*. And denotation is sufficiently indicated by the S; *identity* or *otherness* is indicated by the copula (*is* or *is not*) while *diversity of intension* comes into view only when the Predicate is enunciated. In regard to any assertion, we want to know in the first place *what it is* of which something is affirmed or denied; this knowledge is given with the enunciation of the Subject, which indicates the thing or things spoken of. We want, in the second place, to know *what it is that is affirmed or denied of the thing or things* indicated by the Subject. This information is supplied by the Predicate—that is, by its signification or intension, since it is evident that in affirmative propositions the application of the Predicate is identical with, in negative propositions is altogether distinct from, that of the Subject. Hence it seems clear that in the Predicate of any proposition, it is intension, and not denotation, which is naturally and generally prominent. This is confirmed by the consideration that we commonly use Adjectival Predicates, if appropriate Adjectival Terms are available; and that such terms cannot in English (though they can in many languages) take the sign of the plural, while the Substantive Terms which they qualify can, and no one doubts that the application of an Adjectival Term *is* the same as that of the Substantive Term which it qualifies. Now if it is the primary function of the S in any Categorical Proposition to indicate denotation, while it is the primary function of the P to indicate intension, it seems obvious that quantifying is appropriate, and may be necessary, in the case of S, but not in the case of P, under ordinary circumstances. And a further reason against admitting Quantification (except as a transformation stage) in most propositions, is deducible from the consideration that what propositions affirm or deny is the identity of denotation (in diversity of intension) of S and P; for in a quantificated affirmative, though indeed identity of the terms is still *asserted* (as it is bound to be), the fact that the *denotation* of both terms is made prominent tends to blur this— especially where *difference of extent* of the *classes* referred to is suggested. It might indeed be maintained that where *both* terms of our propositions are taken purely in denotation, quantificated propositions are most appropriate, being the form of proposition which makes the denotation of both S and P most prominent. But both terms *cannot* be taken *purely* in denotation. If, e.g., in *S is P*, both S and P were taken *in denotation only*, then to say *S is P* would be exactly equivalent to saying *S is S*, for the denotation of P is the very same as that of S. On the other hand, the view here advocated of the Import of Categorical Propositions justifies the recognition of Quantification as a phase of propositions. For the Predicates of propositions *have* denotation as well as the Subjects, and (in affirmative propositions) a denotation which is identical with that of the Subjects. It is therefore possible, and under certain conditions allowable and necessary, to make this prominent by quantification. And the Subjects of propositions *have* intension ; and this may be allowed to come into prominence by dropping the sign of quantity which inevitably fixes attention rather upon the denotation than the intension of a term. What Sir Wm Hamilton hoped for from the doctrine of Quanti- fication was, that by its help the relations of classes, as well as the relation of Subject and Predicate, could have been exactly expressed by the form of Assertion. But Quantification is entirely and for ever unequal to the accomplishment of such a task.

The above may be further confirmed and illustrated by a consideration of the traditional logical treatment of O Propositions. Of the four Class Propositions A, E, I, O, the first three have always been regarded as capable, the fourth as incapable, of Conversion.

We have seen that propositions on their way to Conversion have to undergo the process of Quantification. But the reason why O (Some R is not Q) is pronounced inconvertible is not because there is any more difficulty in quantifying its Predicate than in quantificating the other propositions, but because, *when the quantificated converse of O (any Q is not some R) has been reached*, the quantification cannot be dropped without an illegitimate alteration of signification. For the commonly accepted signification of the disquantificated converse of O (Any Q is not R) *implies* a quantification *different from that which has been dropped*—the *dropped* quantification being *some*, the quantification understood as involved in the unquantificated Proposition (Any Q is not R) reached by dropping it, being *any*. And as, at the same time, ordinary thought and speech will not admit the *explicitly quantificated* form, it is inevitable that a Logic which deals with the forms of ordinary thought and speech should regard O as inconvertible. Let us take as a concrete instance the Proposition, Some trees are not oaks (1). This becomes by quantification (2) Some trees are not any oaks, which converts to (3) Any oaks are not some trees. Dropping the quantification of (3), we get (4) Any oaks are not trees, and this would be *understood* to mean (5) Any oaks are not any trees (= No oaks are trees). (*General Logic*, p. 58 &c.)

(1) *All lilies* (S) are *beautiful* (P)
converts to:

(2) *Some beautiful things* (P) are *lilies* (S),
and this again converts to:

(3) *Some lilies* (S) are *beautiful things* (P).

Obviously the quantification *some* in (2) must have been *implicit*, though unexpressed, in (1); and the explicit quantification *some* in (3), must have been implicit in (2).

It is clear that it is the *quantified* Subject and Predicate in Class-Propositions which correspond to the S and P in *S is P*. E.g., in (3) *some lilies* is S, and [*some*] *beautiful things* is P. Similarly with (1) and with (2). If in (1) e.g., the denotation of " beautiful " were not limited to the denotation of "*all lilies*,"—if, that is, *All lilies* (S), were not denotationally identical with only [*some*] *beautiful things* (P), then what the proposition asserts would be identity (of denotation) between *lilies* and *all beautiful things*—an interpretation which is neither intended nor admissible.

(1) No men (S) are angels (P)
converts to:

(2) No angels are men.

Angels was implicitly quantified universally in (1), otherwise the explicit universal quantification of that term-name in (2) would not be possible. By *implicitly quantified* I mean that there is no explicit quantification but that explicit quantification is justified.

In Conversion, as we have been seeing, the Subject-name of the converse is supplied with a sign of quantity which it had not at first, and the Predicate-name of the converse is deprived of the sign of quantity which it originally had.—To sum up: The explanation of this change introduced into Categorical Propositions, when they undergo conversion, is that "the natural way of thinking a Categorical Proposition is to emphasise the extension-aspect in the Subject and the intension-aspect in the Predicate; where an adjective of quantity is expressed, it is inevitable that the aspect of extension should have attention drawn to it. Further, the quantification of the new Subject-name makes clear that this name has had, throughout, an extensive aspect, though that aspect was not emphasised or explicitly brought into notice as long as it was a Predicate-name. The mere transposition of the Predicate into the place of the Subject could not suffice to give it extension unless it had had extension from the beginning, since Conversion is not a legitimate process if it does more than infer something *which is true supposing the inferend is true.*" (*Primer of Logic*, p. 34.)

S is P, S is not P, are susceptible of Obversion, and there is no difficulty in applying this process to Class-Propositions in accordance with the simple procedure applicable to the former. *S is P*, (S P), obverts to *S is not not-P*; *S is not P*, (S ✕ P,) obverts to *S is not-P*.

All robins are insect-eaters,  obverts

to *No robins* (S) are [*any*] *not-insect-eaters* (P) (= All robins are-not not-insect-eaters). Robins being included in the group of insect-eaters, are (by Law of

Excluded Middle) excluded from all those things, whatever

they may be, that do not eat insects:

No painters are mathematicians —(P)(M)— obverts to:

All Painters (S) are not [*any*] *mathematicians* (P).

In inference by Added Determinants of the form: If

R is Q, then X R is Q, ⟮(XR)/Q⟯, it is because the relation
of identity in extension between R and Q remains unaffected by the intension added to the Subject, that we
can add this intension.

E.g. If all ices are unwholesome, then strawberry ices
are unwholesome.

Inference by added Determinants of the form: If
$R = Q$ then $ZR = ZQ$, as applied to quantity or number,
depends on the principle: If equals be added to equals
the wholes are equals.

E.g. If $2 + 2 = 4$ ....(1)
then $2 + 2 + 3 = 4 + 3$ ....(2).

Here there are in (1) two related objects or groups:

$(2+2)$ and (4)

These two are now transformed, by the addition to
each of another object, exactly similar, into objects of
which both denotation and intension have been modified,
but in exactly the same way in both, so that the relation
of equality is maintained.

So, if   40 shillings   = 2 pounds,
then   40 shillings × 4 = 2 pounds × 4.

Again, if £500 will buy one motor,
then £1000 will buy two motors.
Or, if two Northerners can tackle three Southerners,
four Northerners could tackle six Southerners.
I will venture at this point to quote and consider a
passage from a little Logic book[1] which has been reprinted
many times since it was first published in 1870, and is
still largely used in schools and colleges, and recommended
for examinations. The author says: "There are modes
in which all persons do uniformly think and reason, and
must think and reason. Thus if two things are identical
with a third common thing they are identical with each
other. This is a law of thought of a very simple and
obvious character, and we may observe concerning it:

1. That all people think in accordance with it, and
   agree that they do so as soon as they understand its meaning.
2. That they think in accordance with it whatever
   may be the subject about which they are thinking.

Thus if *the things*[2] considered are—
London,
The Metropolis,
The most populous city in Great Britain,
since 'the Metropolis is identical with London,' and
'London is identical with the most populous city in
Great Britain,' it follows necessarily in all minds that
'the Metropolis is identical with the most populous city
in Great Britain.'
Again, if we compare *the three following things*[2]
Iron,
The most useful metal,
The cheapest metal,—

[1] Jevons' *Elementary Lessons in Logic.*   [2] Italics mine.

and it be allowed that 'The most useful metal is Iron,' and 'Iron is the cheapest metal,' it follows necessarily in all minds that 'the most useful metal is the cheapest.'

We here have two examples of *the general truth that things identical with the same thing are identical with each other*[1], and this we may say is a general or necessary form of thought and reasoning.

Compare again the following *three things*[1]—

> The earth,
>
> Planets,
>
> Bodies revolving in elliptic orbits."

As far as I know I am the first person to question this " simple and obvious law of thought," that " if two *things*[1] are identical with a third common *thing*[1] they are identical with each other."   And yet it is not a law either of thought or of things, and it is not simple and obvious,—on the contrary it is untrue and impossible. No *thing* can be identical with any other *thing*: London, The Metropolis, The most populous city in Great Britain, are not three *things*, but *three names* of *one thing*.   If not, we could not say: The Metropolis *is identical with* the most populous city in Great Britain.

The explanation of this passage from Jevons, so chaotic when we come to examine it, is, I suppose, that like so many other thinkers, Jevons, in spite of all his ability and originality, was not clear about the different sorts of *oneness* and *difference,* and (as in his " great rule of inference " the " Substitution of *Similars* ") persistently confused together Identity of Denotation or Extension,

---

[1] Italics mine.   Compare Mansel's interpretation of the Law of Identity.

and Sameness of Intension,—denotative one-ness, and qualitative one-ness. We can no more substitute "similars" in inference than we can "identify" one thing with another thing. "Interchangeability of denotational identicals" would be a much better name for what Jevons means.

Similarity is the category of classing, not of affirmation—this pencil or this stamp may be similar in the highest degree to that, but this is not that. On the other hand, this is "the man who was," but how tragically different. This girl is incredibly like what her grandmother was at 17, but I do not therefore take her for her grandmother, who at 17 was fair and fresh and active, but is now faded and infirm. I have so far learnt to discriminate between cases in which exact similarity is, and those in which it is not, evidence of individual identity.

Similar confusion occurs in a curious form in Mill (*Logic*, I. 116, 9th ed.) when he gives as examples of propositions in which simple Resemblance is asserted the following:

"The colour I saw yesterday was a white colour,"

"The sensation I feel is one of tightness."

Here there seems to be confusion between assertion (*S is P*, identity in diversity) and classing (grouping of this instance with other instances, in virtue of resemblance or similarity), and complete oblivion of anything like a general view of import. We find a like want of clearness in a passage in Jevons' *Elementary Lessons*, p. 65, when he says: "The proposition 'Gold is a yellow substance' states *such an agreement of gold with other yellow substances* that we know it to have the colour yellow," etc.

"Mill tends to drop out of account in his treatment of names and propositions not only all surplusage of intension beyond connotation, but also all explicit reference to the extension aspect. But this—the application of names—is in the very forefront of importance. For Mill, connotation swells and grows till it almost fills the picture, whether we are dealing with Terms or with Import of Propositions. Connotation (where there is Connotation) may *determine* application. But without application somehow determined, all use of names and terms is impossible. Mill himself seems to admit this when he says of Hobbes's definition of Categorical affirmative Propositions ('In every proposition what is signified is the belief of the speaker that the predicate is a name of the same thing of which the subject is a name'), that it is true of all propositions and is the *only* account of import which is rigorously true of all propositions without exception. It is odd that Mill, while setting aside and belittling Hobbes's analysis, should have been content to furnish finally as his own contribution to the theory, nothing better than an analysis (and an exceedingly unsystematic one) of the imports of *different classes of propositions*.

Hobbes, as we have seen, lays all the stress on application of names—on the denotation, not the connotation, aspect—and this carried on into Syllogism would justify the fundamental importance of identity of application of the Middle Term (however this identity may be determined). (Cp. the requirement that the Middle Term in a class syllogism must be 'distributed.') The same would hold of Immediate Inference. And it may be observed that Jevons' doctrine of Substitution of Similars does really lay like emphasis on the supreme part played by application—for the substitution referred to by the 'great rule of inference' which Jevons gives, is Substitution not of 'Similars' but of terms having identical application. The rule runs as follows:

The one supreme rule of inference consists...in the direction to affirm of anything whatever is known of its like, equal or equivalent. The Substitution of Similars is a phrase which seems aptly to express the capacity of mutual replacement existing in any *two objects* which are *like or equivalent* [= ?] to a sufficient [= ?] degree (*Principles of Science*, p. 17, 3rd edit.).

That the substitution here referred to is in fact substitution of terms having identical application is obvious on the most cursory examination, and is apparent at first sight from Jevons' own examples in illustration, e.g.—

(a) Snowdon (1)
    Highest mountain in England or Wales (2)
    (Something) 3590 feet in height (3).

(b) The Lord Chancellor (1)
    The Speaker of the House of Lords (2).

(c) God's image (1)
    Man (2)
    Some reasonable creature (3).

It hardly needs pointing out that in (a) and (c) (1), (2) and (3), and in (b) (1) and (2), respectively, are not qualitative 'similars,' but numerical, historical, or extensional, identicals—intension is in each case *different*, but extension (and therefore application) *the same*. On the other hand, taking things that are so 'similar' as to be intrinsically indistinguishable, we see at once that they cannot be thus 'substituted' the one for the other. 'That house,' e.g., may be similar in the highest degree to another standing next it, but the one *is not* the other, and in inference could not be 'substituted' for it. This copy of Giorgione's 'Richiesta' may be an 'exact' copy, yet could not be 'substituted' for it as The highest mountain in England or Wales could be 'substituted' for Snowdon. One of a pair of twins may be so 'like' the other as to be commonly mistaken for him—yet owing to the one having come into the world a brief space of time before the other, he may be the heir to a dukedom and inheritor of an immense fortune, while the other is neither the one nor the other, and to 'substitute' the one for the other would be inadmissible and even felonious" (*Mind*, 1908, p. 531, etc.).

"When Jevons (*Principles of Science*, ch. III.) discusses the Import, etc., of Categorical Propositions, expressing them as Equations (A = B, etc.), and speaking of them as Identities, I find that some of his examples and some of his explanations are quite in accordance with my analysis. E.g., when he takes the Proposition, *Tower Hill/is/the place where Raleigh was executed*, and says that it 'expresses an identity of place; and whatever is true of the one spot is true of the spot otherwise defined, but in reality the same.' But when he goes on to say that the same analysis can be applied to e.g., the Proposition—

(1) *Colour of Pacific Ocean = Colour of Atlantic Ocean*, finding no distinction between this and e.g.

(2) *Deal = Landing-place of Caesar*, except that in (1) we assert 'identity' of single qualities while in (2) we express 'identity' of groups of qualities, it is clear that there is confusion between extensional and intensional

same-ness. *The colour of the Pacific Ocean* may be *exactly similar to* that of the Atlantic, but we certainly cannot say that the one *is* the other in the sense in which we can say that Deal *is* the place where Caesar landed. This confusion ruins Jevons' whole account of inference, and is even betrayed by the very name-Substitution of *Similars*—which he has chosen to characterise his theory" (*Mind*, 1893, pp. 450, 451).

It would hardly be worth while to take warning examples from Jevons and Mill, if thinkers generally had outgrown this confusion between the different kinds of Same-ness or One-ness which has had such a devastating effect upon theories of import in particular; but there are indications that this is not the case.

For instance, Mrs Ladd Franklin, in discussing the Import of Categoricals, says: "The reason that so many different views are possible is a very simple one. Every term is a double-edged machine—it effects the separating out of a group of objects, and it epitomises a certain complex of marks. From this double nature of the term, it follows...that a proposition which contains two terms must have a fourfold implication....Whoever says, for instance, that 'All politicians are statesmen' must be prepared to maintain that the objects politicians are the same as some of the objects statesmen; and also that the quality-complex politician entails the quality-complex statesman, and is indicative of the presence of some of the objects statesmen....In other words to say that *a* is *b* is to affirm that both from the objects *a* and from the qualities *a* are inferrible both objects *b* and qualities *b*. [But if *a is b*, objects *a* actually *are* objects *b*, and from *qualities a*, *qualities b* need not be inferrible—e.g. a man may be a politician (a) without being a statesman (b)]. Now it is open to the logician to say that any one of these four implications is the most important or the most prominent implication of the proposition, but it is not open to him to say that less than all four of them is the complete implication[1]. *Any one of the four* is a sufficient groundwork on which to work out the entire *system of reasoning*" (*Mind* 1890, p. 561).

By this I believe is meant that we may understand both S and P in denotation, or both in intension (connotation), or S in denotation and P in intension, or S in intension and P in denotation. But when it is said that to affirm *a is b* is to affirm that both from the objects *a* and from the qualities *a*, both objects *b* and qualities *b* are inferrible, I reply that such "inference" is only possible provided we have already understood *a is b* to assert identity of denotation of *a* and *b* (in diversity of intension). As regards the concluding assertion, I proceed shortly to examine "the four" and to show that not one of them is even possible.

Mrs Franklin's view of the "fourfold implication of Propositions in Connotation and Denotation" is approved by Dr Keynes who (in his *Formal Logic*, 3rd ed. p. 147, etc.), expounds the matter as follows:

"(i) If we read the subject of a proposition in denotation and the predicate in connotation, we have what is sometimes called the *predicative mode* of interpreting the proposition. This way of regarding propositions undoubtedly corresponds in the great majority of cases with the course of ordinary thought; that is to say, we

---

[1] Of course the important question is:—*Exactly how* are "all four" *implicated*?

naturally contemplate the subject as a class of objects of which a certain attribute or complex of attributes is predicated " (p. 149).

" (ii) *Subject in denotation, predicate in denotation.*

If we read both the subject and the predicate of a proposition in denotation, we have a relation between two classes, and hence this is called the *class mode* of interpreting the proposition. It must be particularly observed that the relation between the subject and the predicate is now one of *inclusion in* or *exclusion from,* not one of possession. It may at once be admitted that the class mode of interpreting the categorical proposition is neither the most ultimate, nor—generally speaking—that which we naturally or spontaneously adopt. It is, however, extremely convenient for manipulative purposes, and hence is the mode of interpretation usually selected, either explicitly or implicitly, by the formal logician " (p. 151).

" (iii) *Subject in connotation, predicate in connotation.*

If we read both the subject and the predicate of a proposition in connotation, we have what may be called the *connotative mode* of interpreting the proposition. In the proposition *All S is P,* the relation expressed between the attributes connoted by S and those connoted by P is one of *concomitance*—the attributes which constitute the connotation of S are always found accompanied by those which constitute the connotation of P " (p. 154).

" (iv) *Subject in connotation, predicate in denotation.*

Taking the proposition *All S is P,* and reading the subject in connotation and the predicate in denotation, we have—' The attributes connoted by S are an indication of the presence of an individual belonging to the class P.' This mode of interpretation is always a possible one, but it must be granted that only rarely does the import of a proposition naturally present itself to our minds in this form " (p. 146).

I proceed to examine the four readings here recommended to us. (See my article on Logical Judgment in *Mind*, 1893, pp. 452, etc.)

Since, it is said, terms may have Denotation (Extension) or Connotation, or both, any Proposition of the form *S is P* may be read wholly in Denotation, or wholly in Connotation, or S in Denotation and P in Connotation, or S in Connotation and P in Denotation; thus giving four possibilities. If there can be four valid formal theories of Assertion, since each differs considerably from the others it ought no doubt to be possible, as Mrs Ladd Franklin affirms, to have four systems of Logic corresponding to those four theories respectively. It would indeed be interesting to have even the most meagre outline of even one of these four possible theories. But leaving this point, let us look at the alternative readings of *S is P* propositions which are here formulated. That these four alternatives are possible, or indeed that any of them is so, I most emphatically dispute. If the assertion expressed by *S is P* is to be read *wholly* in Extension, (1) then since the Application of S is (by the force of the copula) identical with the Application of P, if we ignore the element of Connotation or Intension (in which alone there is difference) we must express the assertion as *S is S*. *S is not P* is clearly not capable of being even supposably read in Extension only, since diversity of Signification in Subject and Predicate is rendered indispensable by the negative copula.

(2) If *S is P* is to be read in Connotation (or Inten-

sion, or Comprehension) only, again the affirmative *S is P* must melt (cp. Lotze) into *S is S*; for how can *any* connotation be any *other* connotation? If it is said that *S is P* expresses a *combination* of the connotations of S and P, it seems sufficient to point out that the only way in which connotations can be combined is by co-existing in one extension.

Again, if in *S is P* (3) S is taken in Denotation only, and P in Connotation only, or (4) S in Connotation and P in Denotation, what is the force of *is*? *Between what* is Identity supposed to be asserted? We can no more say that Denotation *is* Intension than we can say that This kitten *is* Animality. Is it not plain that, for *is* to have any assertive force, there must be denotational Identity between S and P (in *S is P*), and that for any significance to attach to the assertion, there must be a *diversity* of Connotation or Intension?

In order that e.g., All R (= S) is [some] Q (= P) may be interpreted ("in Extension") to mean:

Class R/is/included in class Q;

or ("in Connotation") to mean:

Attributes R/are/accompanied by Attributes Q;

Class R [some] included in Class Q

not only must both aspects have been taken account of in both Subject and Predicate of the original Proposition but the interpreting Propositions are unintelligible without a similar analysis having been applied to them as they stand, and the interpretations into "in Extension" and "in Connotation" are seen to be entirely founded *not* on the form of the propositions, but on the *intensions* of the subject and predicate. Granted that *All R is [some] Q* (1), may mean *Class R is included in Class Q* (2); this

(2) again has got to be analysed as denotational identity in intensional diversity. Unless so understood, *is* is not admissible, for in intension *Class R* and *included in Class Q* are diverse, we could not say that in intension the one *is* the other. So it is the denotation of *Class R* that is identical with the denotation of the intensionally diverse predicate, [*some*] *included in Class Q*.

The Identity-in-Diversity analysis starts simply and solely from *what is asserted*, the whole (S,P).

And the analysis (identity-in-diversity) being absolutely general and highly abstract, a mere skeleton analysis, admits of further determination of various kinds; the only proviso is, that these further determinations start from and presuppose the skeleton analysis.

E.g. in : All Isosceles Triangles have the angles at the base equal

(= All Isosceles Triangles are having the angles at the base equal),

the identity-in-diversity analysis offers no obstacle to the view that the intension of the Predicate is inseparable from that of the Subject. It allows indeed of this being recognised in the fullest way. In fact the inseparability of the intension of P from that of S quite inevitably involves *identity of denotation* (in diversity of intension).

Mr Russell in *Mind*, 1905, proposes to substitute for Frege's analysis of Categoricals (of which in 1903 he approved) a very complicated statement—e.g. instead of understanding "The father of Charles II was executed" to express identity of denotation (*Bedeutung*) in diversity of intension (*Sinn*), he would interpret it as follows: "It is not always false of x that x begat Charles II, and that x was executed, and that 'If y begat Charles II, y is identical with x' is always true of y" (p. 482).

As regards this I would point out that in my view (1) the speaker who asserts that *The Father of Charles II was executed* starts from the subject-matter of assertion,

the complex whole: (Father of Charles II Executed) and in order to deal in

any way with this, it has to be first of all analysed on the identity in diversity plan, so that "Father of Charles II" and "executed" are referred to the denotation of the subject as its intension. (2) The statement: "It is not always false of x, etc." involves several repetitions of identity in diversity:

(a) It is not always false of x, (b) that x begat Charles II and that (c) x was executed, and that (d) if y begat Charles II, (e) y is identical with x, (f) is always true of y.

Unless these clauses are to be understood as identities-in-diversity, what can be made of them, what is the connexion between their elements? I understand that Mr Russell's object in giving up Frege's view and putting forward this complicated substitute, is to eliminate "denoting phrases" and so get rid of inconvenient implications of "existence." But he does not seem to have escaped identity of denotation in diversity of intension (in the ordinary sense of denotation and intension)—and I cannot avoid the conviction that any *form* of proposition is incapable of determining questions of "existence," just as much as forms of proposition (S *is* P, etc.) are incapable of completely and determinately expressing relations of classes.

In: All Cavicornia are Ruminants,
    All Antelopes are Cavicornia,
    All Antelopes are Ruminants,

the relation of Terms may be diagrammatically represented thus:

The true Middle Term is the *some Cavicornia* of the Minor Premiss; for it is only that part of the denotation of Cavicornia which is common to both Antelopes and Ruminants, that is the bond of connexion between them. The Ruminants that Antelopes are, are the Ruminants whose denotation is identical with that of those Cavicornia that are identical with Antelopes. Of those Ruminants whose denotation does not coincide with that of any Cavicornia, and of those Cavicornia whose denotation does not coincide with that of any Antelopes, it must be said that they are not Antelopes, and that Antelopes are not they. It is the indefiniteness of the *some* by which Ruminants in the Major Premiss, and Cavicornia in the Minor Premiss are implicitly quantified, that makes it necessary to sweep in the whole extension of Cavicornia, so as to make sure that those Cavicornia with which (as being Antelopes) we are concerned, are Ruminants.

Sameness of Denotation (identity) of Middle Term in Mediate Inference is that which connexion between Major and Minor Terms must depend upon, for it cannot depend on sameness of intension or exact similarity (cp. Jevons' " Substitution of *Similars* "); *intensional* sameness, the closest similarity, would not justify substitution—if it would, there would be no reason why the Middle Term in a Syllogism should be distributed—the *intension* M would be all that could be required as a link, and (as in all S is M, all P is M), S might be identified with one part of the Class M, and P with another part, and as a result S identified with P, which is absurd,

In:

      No diamonds are red

      This stone is red.

∴ This stone is not a diamond.

      No diamonds = *P*

      [*any*] and [*some*] *red* = *M*.

      This stone = S

      Some red is, denotationally, part of *any red*.

In:

      All sapphires are blue

      This stone is not blue.

∴ This stone is not a sapphire.

      All sapphires = P

      [*any*] and [*some*] *blue = M*.

      This stone = S

      Some blue is identical with part of *any blue.*

It is *some red* and *some blue* which are the true middle terms. Compare the account of the "Antelope" syllogism above.

It is because Class relations as expressed in the A, I, O forms are indeterminate, that in Mediate Inference we cannot make the Terms correspond exactly with the clear and perfectly definite forms of the *S is P, S is not P* type when we are dealing with unquantified class-syllogisms.

This may be done however in the case of what has been called Traduction, where all the subjects are singular and have identical denotation, e.g.

London is the largest city in the world,

London is the capital of England,

The capital of England is the largest city in the world.

London: Capital of England: Largest city

It is done exactly in every Mediate Inference (Traductional or other) in which the denotations of all the Terms are determinate, e.g.

Syndics and Night Watch Two of R.'s masterpieces Two of the pictures in the New Museum

The Syndics and Night Watch are two of Rembrandt's masterpieces;

The Syndics and Night Watch are two of the pictures in the New Museum at Amsterdam;

Two of the pictures in the New Museum are two of Rembrandt's masterpieces.

It seems unnecessary here to consider the differences of Syllogistic Figure, and of Mood in as far as variation of Mood in Class-Propositions goes beyond the three cases possible when we use the *S is P, S is not P* forms only—

i.e.

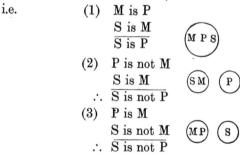

(1)   M is P
      $\dfrac{\text{S is M}}{\text{S is P}}$ (M P S)

(2)   P is not M
      $\dfrac{\text{S is M}}{\therefore\ \text{S is not P}}$ (S M)   (P)

(3)   P is M
      $\dfrac{\text{S is not M}}{\therefore\ \text{S is not P}}$ (M P)   (S)

Such differences of Mood and Figure may result from the indeterminateness of A, I, O, and further variations of determination due to the fact that the *some* of explicit quantification is itself indeterminate. If we allow conversion of Class-Propositions to be possible, we must admit that in every case the Terms are either explicitly or implicitly quantified; owing to the conventions of customary speech, the quantification is generally implicit; when made explicit it is mostly indeterminate; but its possibility is incontestable proof of the denotation of Predicates. If in affirmative Categoricals it were possible (which it is not) to simply add the intension of the Predicate to the denotation of the Subject, we should avoid all difficulties due to the implicit *some* and the indeterminateness of denotation of Predicate; but then the Propositions would be incapable of Conversion.

An examination of concrete Hypothetical, Conditional, and Disjunctive (Alternative) Propositions shows that here too the analysis of Categorical Affirmation as identity of denotation in diversity of intension is applicable. Take the following Conditionals: If any child is spoilt, he is troublesome, asserts the identity of denotation of *spoilt child* with *troublesome child*.

If any rose is blue, it is a curiosity, asserts denotational identity of Blue Rose with a Curiosity.

Take the following Hypotheticals, of which (1) is Self-contained, i.e. the consequent is a necessary consequence of the antecedent taken alone:

(1) If all men are fallible and the Archbishop is a man, the Archbishop is fallible.

What is asserted is, that granting that the denotation  of man is part of the denotation of fallible, and that the denotation of the Archbishop is part of the denotation of man, then it follows that the denotation of Archbishop is part of the denotation of fallible.

(2) If Charles I had not deserted Strafford, he would be deserving of sympathy.

This asserts that supposing denotation of Charles I to be identical with denotation of one who did not desert Strafford, then (because not to have deserted Strafford would have been to deserve sympathy) the denotation of Charles I would have been the denotation of one deserving of sympathy. In this example it is not from the expressed antecedent alone that the consequence follows, but from that antecedent taken in conjunction with another (unexpressed) proposition.

(3) If the building goes on, he will not recover.

This may be expanded into :

If the work goes on, great noise will be made ;

If great noise is made, he will be disturbed by it ;

If he is disturbed, he will not sleep ;

If he does not sleep, he will die.

The conclusion *he will die* results from a series of suppositions in which building going on (1) is identified (denotationally) with making noise (2), making noise with disturbing him (3), disturbing him with preventing his sleeping (4), preventing his sleeping with preventing his recovery (5). What holds the argument together deno-

tationally is just as much of the denotations of (2), (3),
(4) and (5) as are identical with
the denotation of (1). (This is not
affected by the circumstance that
here denotational identities follow
from intensional connexions).

The efficacy of the identity-
in-diversity analysis is I think
nowhere more strikingly seen than
in its application to Hypotheticals,
especially Hypotheticals of the elliptical and often complicated sort which we so commonly employ, and of which
the illustrations (2) and (3) examined above are instances.

I will here take as one more illustration, Lewis
Carroll's " Logical Paradox," the discussion of which has
at intervals amused the readers of *Mind* since 1894[1].
The case presented by Lewis Carroll is, that in a certain
barber's shop there are three attendants, Allen, Brown
and Carr, and at no time are they all out together,
i.e. Allen or Brown or Carr is always in (1). According
to this we may have A, B and C all in, only A and B in,
only A and C in, only B and C in (a), only A in, only B
in (b), or only C in; and
(1) all times are times at
which one man is in. But
(2) if Allen is out Brown
is out (because Allen
has been ill and cannot
go out without Brown).

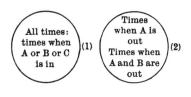

So (a) B and C are in and Allen is out, and
    (b) B is in and Allen and Carr are out, are in-

admissible cases—(a) is barred by (2) because A is out implies B is out (= All times that Allen is out are times that Brown is out). So Brown and Carr cannot be in when Allen is out. And Allen is out = Allen and Brown are both out (by (2)).

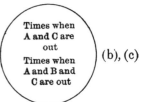

Times when A and C are out
Times when A and B and C are out

(b), (c)

So in (b) Carr and Allen are out = Carr and Allen and Brown are out (c), and by (1) All times are times when A or B or C is in. So (b) as it stands is barred by (2), and as amended to (c), is barred by (1).

The interest of this analysis of Lewis Carroll's instance is that the whole case is subject to two conditions:

(1)   That A or B or C must always be in;

(2)   That A cannot be out without B; and these may conflict, and it is not easy at first sight to see exactly how to combine the fulfilment of both conditions, and exactly what denotational identities are justified by the combination.   As in all elliptical Hypotheticals, when the argument is expanded to a full statement the *whole conditions* need to be explicitly taken account of; and as has been indicated, the whole argument in any case may be completely set out in a series of propositions asserting identity-in-diversity[1].

In any concrete case in which it is possible to assert that:

If A is true, the truth of C follows,

If A is true, the truth of C does not follow,

it will be found on examination that either each Hypothetical is elliptical or A is itself contradictory.

[1] An interesting solution of Lewis Carroll's "Paradox" is offered by Mr Bertrand Russell in *Mind* for 1905 (pp. 400, 401).   He says that he

E.g. in:

If this is Inference, the conclusion is contained in the premisses;

If this is Inference, the conclusion goes beyond the premisses,

it is clear that the Hypotheticals are elliptical.

Disjunctive (or Alternative) Propositions are equivalent to Hypotheticals or Conditionals, and may be analysed in the same way.

E.g. Any topaz is pink or yellow

= Any topaz is pink or (if not pink) is yellow

= If any topaz is not pink, it is yellow.

They must come some other time than Saturday afternoon or I cannot receive them, may mean:

Saturday afternoon is a time when I shall be away from home;

---

considers the paradox to be "a good illustration of the principle that a false proposition implies every proposition. Putting p for 'Carr is out,' q for 'Allen is out,' and r for 'Brown is out,' Lewis Carroll's two Hypotheticals are:—

(1) q implies r.

(2) p implies that q implies not-r.

Lewis Carroll supposes that 'q implies r' and 'q implies not-r' are inconsistent, and hence infers that p must be false. But as a matter of fact 'q implies r' and 'q implies not-r' must both be true if q is false, and are by no means inconsistent. Thus the only inference from Lewis Carroll's premisses (1) and (2) is that if p is true, q is false, i.e. that if Carr is out, Allen is in. This is the complete solution of the paradox."

But (i) if q implies r and q implies not-r are *not* inconsistent, *how do we know* (on the above reasoning) that q is false? (ii) We seem to admit here both that the truth of q implies r (1), and also that the falsity of q implies r. (iii) In (1) q implies r unconditionally, in (2) the implication is conditional on the truth of p.

A time when I shall be away from home is a time
when I cannot receive visitors;
If they come on Saturday afternoon they come at a time
when I cannot receive visitors.

In regard to the interpretation of
Alternative Propositions, the one question in dispute regarding the alter-
nants of the proposition is: Are they exclusive or un-
exclusive? Though there has been great division of
opinion among logicians on this point, and though there
are Alternative Propositions such as: "He came in either
second or third," "We start either Wednesday or Thurs-
day," in which it is quite clear that while we cannot deny
both alternatives, neither can we assert both, yet there
can be no doubt that in such cases the exclusiveness of
the alternatives is due not to the form of proposition,
but to the nature of the cases in question. "It thus
seems that the only account which we can give of the
general or *formal* import of Alternatives—that is to say
of the import which is *common to every one of them*—
is that if we deny one alternative, we must affirm the
other. It should be observed that although terms used
as alternatives are not necessarily exclusive in extension
or denotation, they *are* exclusive in intension, in as far as
they are not tautologous (in which case the alternation
seems to vanish). Thus, in 'All his parishioners are
criminals or paupers,' the alternatives, though not denotationally exclusive—since the same parishioner may be
both criminal and pauper—are necessarily exclusive intensionally, since we cannot say that they are synonymous."
(*Primer of Logic*, p. 26.)

As regards the doctrine of Opposition, it is of particular interest from my point of view, because on the
identity-in-diversity analysis it presents in a clear com-
pact form the equation of the fivefold class-relation to
the traditional fourfold schedule of class-propositions.
Any two classes indicated by intension or by symbols
may have one of five extensional relations to each other.
Let us take R and Q to symbolise two classes.   The
scheme may then be set out as follows:

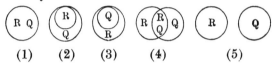

(1)   (2)   (3)   (4)   (5)

A.   All R is Q = (1) or (2).
E.   No R is Q = (5).
I.   Some R is Q : (1) or (2) or (3) or (4).
O.   Some R is not Q = (3) or (4) or (5).

Of these propositions A and E may both be false, but
they cannot both be true; I and O may both be true,
but they cannot both be false; of A and O, and of E
and I, one is true and the other false.   If A is true, I is
true, if I is false, A is false; if E is true, O is true; if
O is false, E is false.   Reference to the diagrams makes
the whole scheme at once self-evident, and the diagrams
exhibit the identity or non-identity of Subject and Predicate in every case.   To take concrete examples of Contra-
dictories (A and O, E and I), we may say:

Either all beliefs are true ((1) or (2)), or some are
not true ((3) or (4) or (5)).

Either no men are perfectly happy ((5)), or some are
so ((1) or (2) or (3) or (4)).

Conditionals come under the same rule as Cate-

goricals in respect of Opposition, and any proposition of
the form : *If A, then C,* contraposits to *If not-C, then not-A,*
and may be contradicted by : the
truth of C does not follow from
the truth of A—i.e. though A is
true C is doubtful (which exactly
expresses the relation between I
and A, O and E). To take a
concrete case :

   (1) If money go before,
all ways lie open,
may be contradicted
by :

   (2) Though money go be-
fore, it does not follow that all ways lie
open. (*Primer of Logic,* p. 37.)

The Identity of Denotation in Diversity of Intension
analysis applies whether we are considering what is
asserted ; or the assertor—the speaker or teacher—who
starts from the whole (S P) ; or the hearer or learner, who
receives the assertion piecemeal, and *finishes* with the
whole.

The two different attitudes afford some explanation of
different theories of import of propositions, etc. It is
plain, e.g., that the account of judging according to which
it consists in putting two ideas together, and the Canons
of Syllogism: (1) Two terms agreeing with one and the
same third term agree with each other, (2) two terms
of which one agrees and the other does not agree with
one and the same third term, do not agree with each
other: are adapted to the point of view of hearer or

learner; while the view of Brentano and Hillebrand, that in any judgment *S is P*, one object 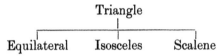 is present to the mind, is evidently appropriate to the point of view of teacher or speaker—the hearer has to *build up* the whole —he reaches it in the end, he does not start from it.

The speaker who has before him a whole composed of parts of denotation—e.g. a division or classification of Triangle, thus:

Triangle

Equilateral   Isosceles   Scalene

or a clockmaker with a clock, or a schoolboy with a knife, or an astronomer contemplating the planetary system, or a General in a campaign with a plan of operations sketched out in his mind—all these can communicate to others piecemeal as much as they wish of that which is cognised by them, by means of propositions of the forms *S is P*, *S is not P*. No doubt if they can set before their audience the actual table of classification, the actual piece of mechanism, the actual knife, a working model of a planetary system and so on, the exposition is immensely helped, or may even be rendered unnecessary. Of course such helps are used in teaching wherever possible— blackboard-drawings, models, lantern slides, etc.

The difficulties of (1) impersonal and (2) elliptical propositions, such as (1) It rains, (2) Fire! Wolf! are very much mitigated if it is remembered that in every case the speaker must start, not from the words of his pronouncement, but from the matter of fact, not from the expressed assertion, but from *what is asserted*. The corre-

spondence of the verbal assertion to *that which it asserts*
is often regarded as artificial, and the verbal expression is
called a "verbal device," or by some name that has an
equally opprobrious implication. Of course it cannot be
denied that if I have before me a *red rose* and assert:
This rose is red, my spoken assertion consists entirely of
words, and in particular contains a copula to which *the
red rose* seems to present nothing even remotely corre-
spondent. Accordingly some logicians wish to reject the
copula, and some think it a verbal device in the very
worst sense, a useless, embarrassing and unjustified re-
dundancy of expression. From my point of view, however, all this is mistaken. If what is asserted in any
S is P is identity of denotation in diversity of intension,
then in asserting it we want not only the diverse terms
with their intensions and denotations, but also something
which indicates and conveys to the hearer the identity
of denotation between the terms, and this function the
copula is admirably fitted to perform. And the negative
copula is just as well suited to its particular task. In
fact the copula seems to me a very economical and
effective means of carrying out a delicate and indispensable part of the whole function of communicating by
means of speech. It is one of the many instances in
which men "have builded better than they knew."

In such propositions as: The round-square is non-
existent, we cannot dispense with a one-ness of denotation
(extension) in the subject, because, without this, *round*
and *square* would have simply their intensional diversity
—there would be no even hypothetical joining together of
round and *square*, no problem, no difficulty, no reason to
assert "non-existence," to raise any question. Since in

space, as known to us, roundness cannot be square, and squareness cannot be round, the denotation to which the two qualifications are assigned can "exist" only in the universe (or region) of hypothesis or supposition. This hypothetical combination is denied a place in the "universe" of actual space.

Where intensions, attributes, are (1) incompatible, or (2) inseparable, then the attempt (1) to combine them in one subject, one denotation, as round-square, or (2) to separate them, as equiangularity from equilaterality in a triangle, is an attempt which can never be realised. We may "suppose" the conjunction (or separation), we can assert it, and trace its consequences, but that is all,—as I might suppose that I could fly like an eagle, swim like a fish, and be stronger than an elephant, and deduce various things that I could do on these suppositions.

In using impossible combinations as Subjects (or Predicates) of Propositions, or a Subject which has a Predicate which cannot co-inhere with it in one denotation, we are perhaps sometimes simply extending forms and processes of language, appropriate in some cases, to cases to which they are not primarily and directly applicable.

Suppose I say:

No roses are blue $\left(R\right)\left(B\right)$,

this may be expressed also as:

There are no blue roses, or Blue roses = 0, or
Blue roses are non-existent.

All these seem admissible ways of expressing the matter of fact indicated by the diagram $\left(R\right)\left(B\right)$.

Apply this to the round-square case :

(1)   No squares are round (S) (R) .

There are no round-squares.

Round-squares = 0.

Round-squares are non-existent.

Even on this view, however, we have to postulate the conjunction of round and square in a suppositional denotation.

In speaking of Squares and Rounds in (1), we are naturally understood to be referring to the region or universe of space as known to us, by Rounds and Squares we mean plane figures of a definite familiar shape.

But when we say *Round-squares do not exist* we assign only our *Predicate* to that same extended universe, and the Subject which is *round and square* belongs to a region of the merest, and we may even say wildest, hypothesis—a region entirely separate from the region in which squares that are merely square, and rounds that are simply round, have their "existence." The round-squares are declared to be non-existent, they are identified (in denotation) with something that is non-existent.

But that non-existence does not signify complete and unmitigated non-existence, but only the absence of spatial existence—in talking about round-squares we are talking about *something*, although it is an incoherent and unrealisable something.

Whatever is thought of as having denotation, is thereby thought of as having "being," existence of some sort, of *what* sort has to be fixed by intensional determination.

All the wheels that go to Croyland are shod with silver, was a picturesque way of saying that no ordinary work-a-day wheels did ever go to Croyland. The wheels that went there were shod with silver, that is to say, they belonged to the same region as silver-shod wheels, viz., the region of imagination—shod with india-rubber would probably have been an even more far-fetched idea, at the time when the saying was framed—but fens have been drained and roads constructed, no doubt the rubber tyres of motors have found their way to the ruins of the ancient abbey, and it might some day occur to a cranky millionaire going in that direction to have the tyres of his wheels of silver metal—now so much less precious than formerly,— if only to illustrate the legend.

" Existence " of some sort we must attribute to every-thing of which we speak. But no particular kind of existence can be implied by forms (such as *S is P*) which propositions that deal both with the "real" world and with mere fancy or fiction, have in common. The *kind* of existence anything has is shown by the predicates we can give it. Any proposition *S is P* that I assert, is an entity, has some sort of existence. But the important question is, *What* sort ? Is it *true*, for instance ? Well, this must be tested by criteria. I cannot doubt (1) what is self-evident, as that a whole is greater than its part ; or (2) what is to me matter of direct experience, as that that flash of lightning was followed by a clap of thunder ; or (3) what is logically deduced from that which is accepted as true, e.g. if twenty shillings are equal to £1, forty shillings are equal to £2 ; or (4) what is in harmony with all which I accept, as that parallel lines do

not enclose a space; or (5) that which is implied in what
is accepted as true—e.g. that propositions of the form
S is P (*S is not P*)—(by the help of which alone the
Laws of Contradiction and Excluded Middle can be
asserted, and in which, in fact, most of our assertions,
whether self-evident or disputable, must be affirmed or
denied, supported or called in question)—that propositions of these forms are possible and valid.

As already insisted on, what *S is P* asserts, is that the
denotation of S, whatever it is, is the denotation of P.
If we start with an S which has not any denotation to
begin with, nothing can ever bestow that which is lacking.
But of what sort the denotation of S is, is settled by its
intension, and the intension of its predicate, and by context,
as in the old-fashioned school-room game in which one
person thinks of a thing, and another person has to try
and find out what it is by asking questions, to which the
answer must be *Yes* or *No*. The thing questioned about
is thought of by the questioner as being something, as
having some existence, but of what sort it is, in what
region it is, is revealed to him only when he knows what
predicates, what intension, can be assigned to it. As to
" Real" Existence, it is subject to as much ambiguity as
Identity is, and the ambiguity in this case is far more
difficult to clear up. How are we to define or describe
Reality? What about the future, what about the past?
The roses that have faded and fallen this year, and those
that will blossom next year? What about ideas of the
non-existent, which become operative in the world of
Time and Matter?

What are we to say of the ideal of an architect, painter,
poet, novelist, reformer, which guides the action of the man,

and leads to physically embodied results which may be widely influential? Or even of the delusions of a madman, which are intensely "real" to him and may lead him to realise the most disastrous actions in the everyday world of space and time? I remember reading a tragic story of the Captain of a ship who on a voyage went out of his mind. He fell under the delusion that various members of the crew were conspiring to mutiny, and with marvellous caution and cunning, induced 'first one and then another of the officers and men to share his suspicions of some of their number, and help him to secure them. He succeeded so well that most of the crew (it was not a large one) were overpowered one by one, and bound and made helpless. Then, having laid all his plans with superhuman ingenuity, with the strength and fury of a madman and armed with weapons which he had secreted, he fell upon the unfortunate victims, and the ship arrived in port with the Captain a raging lunatic and most of the crew murdered. What view are we to take of "reality" in such a case?

Or again of the perverted judgment of a dipsomaniac, or of such a mother as the one in *The Green Graves of Balgowrie*, which leads to cruel ill-treatment of the children of the person so afflicted; or the "fixed idea" of an old-fashioned miser who leaves his unfortunate sons and daughters half-starved and uneducated, to save a lawyer's fee, draws his own will, with the result that it does not carry out his intentions, and himself dies of starvation.

The finding of the North Pole by Dr Cook, and the near approach to the South Pole by Lieutenant Shackleton were, some months ago, on the same level of "reality" as far as the general public knew, and neither achievement could have been even discussed or questioned, unless it had been provisionally credited with "denotation," "existence," or "reality," in the region at least of supposition. We identify the denotation of P with the denotation of S just the same whether we merely suppose *S is P*, or question it, or affirm it, or consciously suspend our judgment.

The reproach of unreality is, it would seem, only pertinent when one kind of reality is mistakenly identified with another kind.

I hope that I have in the foregoing pages made good my undertaking, and shown that the substitution for the old Law of Identity, *A is A*, of the principle that Every Subject of Predication is an Identity (of Denotation) in Diversity (of Intension), does provide the explicit recognition and justification of *S is P*, *S is not P* propositions which Logic has hitherto needed but not had, and does furnish Formal Logic with a real and obvious basis, and an adequate constructive principle.

My scheme, I hold, elucidates (among other things) the relations of Denotation (Extension) and Intension; the general Import of Categorical Propositions and their relation to Conditionals, Hypotheticals and Alternatives; Immediate and Mediate Inference; the relations to each other, and to logical science, of the three Laws of Thought; the meaning and place of Quantification; the general relation between Relative and Non-relative Propositions; the fundamental difference between the relation of Subject and Predicate in Assertion and other relations which have been sometimes confounded with it—e.g. the relations of

(1) Subject (Substance) and Attribute, and (2) relations of Classes; the difference between extensional one-ness, and qualitative one-ness.

On my principles, as I think, the whole of Formal Logic becomes a systematised and harmonious whole, with a sound basis, an obvious and all-pervading principle, and a simple and coherent structure.

FALLACIES.

It remains to say a word about Fallacies—Fallacies may be brought into a simple connexion with the Identity in Diversity analysis of Categoricals by the consideration that all fallacy consists in either identifying what is distinct or distinguishing what is identical, so that we get a primary division of Fallacies into (a) those of *mistaken distinction*, which are Fallacies of Tautology, and (b) those of *mistaken identification*, which are Fallacies in which there is failure of continuity, and may be called Fallacies of Discontinuity. The classification possible on these lines is summed up in the following Table. (See *Primer of Logic*.)

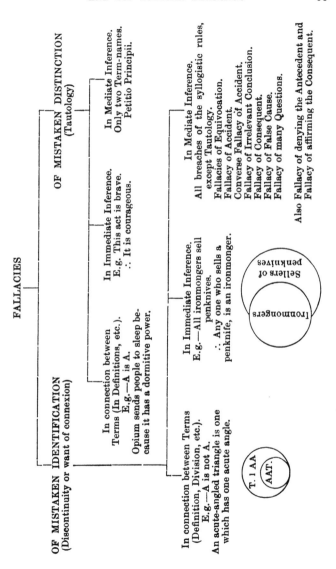

FALLACIES

OF MISTAKEN IDENTIFICATION
(Discontinuity or want of connexion)

OF MISTAKEN DISTINCTION
(Tautology)

In connection between Terms
(Definition, Division, etc.).
E.g.—A is not A.
An acute-angled triangle is one
which has one acute angle.

In connection between
Terms (In Definitions, etc.).
E.g.—A is A.
Opium sends people to sleep be-
cause it has a dormitive power.

In Immediate Inference.
E.g.—All ironmongers sell
penknives.
∴ Any one who sells a
penknife, is an ironmonger.

In Immediate Inference.
E.g. This act is brave.
∴ It is courageous.

In Mediate Inference.
Only two Term-names.
Petitio Principii.

In Mediate Inference.
All breaches of the syllogistic rules,
except Tautology.
Fallacies of Equivocation.
Fallacy of Accident.
Converse Fallacy of Accident.
Fallacy of Irrelevant Conclusion.
Fallacy of Consequent.
Fallacy of False Cause.
Fallacy of many Questions.

Also Fallacy of denying the Antecedent and
Fallacy of affirming the Consequent.

DEFINITIONS OF CERTAIN TERMS.

Proposition
Assertion } I use in the same sense, as denoting the
statements of Categorical, Inferential (Hypothetical), or
Alternative form, e.g. S is P; If A is B, C is D; C is D
or A is not B. In as far as the words in an assertion can
be considered apart from *what is asserted* I would use the
name *verbal expression*—or, if more convenient, *sentence*.

By *what is asserted* (or the *assertum*) I mean that
matter of fact, or belief, or state of the case, which the
assertion or proposition sets forth in words. The speaker
apprehends, or is conscious of, something which he conveys
by means of words to his audience; that *something* is *what
is asserted*,—e.g. he sees the door open and conveys the
fact in the assertion: "The door is open"; or he is aware
of feeling very chilly, and conveys the fact by asserting
the proposition: "I am chilled to the bone," or he believes
that "Twice two is four" and asserts it. The assertion
or proposition is of course a "verbal device"—(though
a necessary and indeed an indispensable one)—and in
particular the copula is sometimes accused of being a
device in a specially bad sense and of having nothing
corresponding to it in what is asserted. Such objections
seem beside the mark—no one attempts to deny the
difference between *what is asserted* and *the assertion of
it*—the point is: Does the assertion made by the speaker
convey to the hearer a knowledge of what the speaker
asserts? If so, it answers its purpose fully and perfectly.
The copula in particular seems to me one of the most
admirable of human devices—briefly and simply and

modestly helping to fulfil the function of conveying to every hearer the information, the matter of fact, the somewhat asserted, which any speaker desires to communicate.

The distinction which I draw between the attitude of speaker or teacher on the one hand, and hearer or learner or seeker on the other, which is of great interest and importance in Logic, seems to be specially enlightening here.

Denotation (Extension) of a term means the sphere of its application—the things of which the term is the name, the things to which the term applies.

Intension of a term means the properties of the things to which the term applies—it "may be used to indicate in the most general way the implicational aspect of name" (Keynes).

Connotation is that part of the Intension of a Term which is set out in the Definition, and on account of which the name is applicable.

Sameness = (1) one-ness of denotation, identity; (2) similarity, resemblance, likeness, qualitative one-ness (Same-ness might conveniently be restricted to qualitative one-ness).

Identity = denotational one-ness, existential or extensional unity—antithetic to Distinctness, Otherness. Compare "mistaken identity."

One-ness = antithetic to Difference =
    (1) denotational one-ness, identity;
    (2) qualitative one-ness, same-ness.

Unity = (1) Identity, (2) Same-ness, (3) any system, or whole made up of parts, and (4) the relation between such parts.

Difference = (1) Distinctness or Otherness, such as the difference between *this new shilling* and *that new shilling* of the same minting; (2) Diversity—e.g. such a difference as there is between justice and generosity, humanity and mortality, or between an egg and the robin into which it hatches; (3) (Differentia) the characteristics by which any sub-Class (or species) is distinguished (differenced) from the rest of its wider containing class (or Genus).

Diversity—see Difference.

Distinctness—see Difference.

Otherness—see Difference. (Compare: give me *another*, give me a *different* one.)

Similarity. There is similarity between *two* things when they resemble each other—produce impressions which we call *like*; and there is similarity between the different phases of one thing *in so far* as it remains unaltered. Similarity may be slight and partial, or so great as to amount to what has been called *indistinguishable resemblance* (= qualitative one-ness). Similarity (Resemblance) is antithetic to *Diversity*.

The phrase *exact similarity* as equivalent to qualitative one-ness is sometimes objected to on the ground that, e.g., squareness or snow-whiteness or mortality have extensional as well as intensional one-ness—that the mortality of Socrates is *identical* with the mortality of Newton—or even that extensional and intensional one-ness in such cases coalesce—or are indistinguishable—This appears to involve a monadistic existence of qualitative or conceptual entities. I think that granting such entities if we could assert of any one of them, S, that it is P, we could not do this without postulating or implying that it is an identity-in-diversity. For S is given as intensionally diverse from P—that is, intensionally S is not P. If, therefore, S is P, the one-ness indicated must be something different from intensional one-ness. It must be a one-ness of being to which the diverse intensions are referred—that is an extensional one-ness. Under no other condition can one-ness of intensional diversity be asserted. Even in the case of, e.g., obtuse-angled triangularity, we cannot say that Triangularity is Obtuse-angled-ness, but only that a triangle may be obtuse-angled.

The relation of Identity-in-Diversity of Subject and Predicate in Predication (1) must be distinguished from

(2) relation of Subject and Attribute (the subject of Predication may be the attribute of a Subject (Substance)—e.g. Triangularity is a property of plane figures).

(3) From relations of classes. Relation of S and P in Predication is twofold only—either (a) a relation of identity or coincidence (of denotation or extension) or (b) a relation of denotational exclusion, while the relations possible between two classes are five.

(4) From the relation of successive similar percepts to a conception or general notion which is implicated in every general name. When Mill says that the import of such propositions as: The colour I saw yesterday was a white colour, The sensation I feel is one of tightness, is to *assert* resemblance, he seems to confuse (1) with (4). If his account of the import of these two propositions is correct, then *every* proposition which has a general name for Predicate is a proposition "asserting" Resemblance, e.g. Rosa is fair-haired, This orange is ripe, Arsenic is a cause of death.

(5) From the relation of members of a class (a) to each other or (b) to the class.

Identical. Used to mean denotationally the same, the same individual or thing.

System. By System is meant a group of two or more related objects or items.

Logical Inference. When we can say that

If a proposition (or pair of propositions) A is true, another proposition C is true;

then C is a logical inference (eductive or deductive) from A—that is, the truth of C is implied in the truth of A, we cannot affirm C and deny A, C follows from A.

Logical Inference has to be distinguished from Instinctive or "Psychological" Inference, and from what may be called Tentative Inference, which may be (1) a sudden *aperçu*, a revelation, an intuition, or (2) an Hypothesis or guess, deliberately framed for purposes of investigation. "If we take the simplest possible case of mediate inference or syllogism (Deduction) we have *S is M, M is P*, entitling us to the inference *S is P*. Here we have, no doubt, as the conclusion, an assertion or proposition, which (*quâ* assertion or proposition) differs in some way from either of the premisses; or from both taken together. At the same time the content of the assertion *S is P* is certainly in some way contained in and justified by *M is P* and *S is M*. The exact connexion seems to me to be as follows: When as audience or seeker or pupil, we have learnt that *M is P* and *S is M*, and grasped the contents of the two assertions and their connexion, we find that we have really produced a construction in which the connotations or intensions S and M and P are referred to one denotation (s,m,p). Having this whole before us as an object of thought, or imagination, it is apparent that it entitles us to say not only that *S is M* and *M is P*, but also that *S is P*, and even further, if we wish, that *P is M* and *M is S* and *P is S*, *Not-P is not M, not-M is not S*, etc. The same might be shown in a similar though even simpler way, of any case of Immediate Inference (Eduction).

We may, of course, syllogise and otherwise 'infer' in an unintelligent mechanical way, using the accepted laws of Formal Inference and of the 'Systems' concerned as mere 'rules of thumb,' guides blindly obeyed. But if the acceptance of these rules can be justified, it must be seen that they are valid. It is, e.g., the vision actual or possible of a constructed whole, S that is M, M that is P,

(s,m,p) that justifies to our mind the assertion of (among other statements) S is P as an inference from *S is M* and *M is P*.

I believe that a clear distinction between the contrasted attitudes of hearer, reader, or learner on the one hand, and speaker or teacher on the other hand, is very important indeed for the theory of Logical Inference." (See *Mind*, 1908, pp. 533, 534.)